STRENGTH IN SCARS

PAIN, PRISON, AND THE DRUNK DRIVER WHO
CHANGED EVERYTHING

SYDNEY MICKEY

The Cover and Symbolism

My favourite colour is pink, mine and Kayden's (son) Indigenous crest is a Laxgibuu (lucky-boo, wolf), Shane's (boyfriend) was a Ganhada (gan-hadda, raven), lady bugs have always been a symbol to my fam as the women in our family who have passed away. Eagles and ravens are a symbol of the male loved ones who have passed away.

SYDNEY MICKEY

CONTENTS

INTRODUCTION

When I first read Sydney's story, I didn't just read words; I felt them. Every sentence carried the heartbeat of a warrior who refused to surrender.

Her life is a map of mountains climbed, falls survived, and a spirit reclaimed.

As the founder of Women Like Me, I've had the honor of reading hundreds of stories of survival, but Sydney's story left me breathless.

It is not just about the pain of growing up in generational trauma, or the horror of a single moment that changed everything.

It's about rebirth, about reclaiming a body, a voice, and a life that the world once tried to take.

Sydney writes not from a place of pity but of power. She carries her scars like medals of truth, shining proof that strength can be rebuilt from the rubble.

Through every heartbreak, every relapse, every small victory, she teaches us what it means to rise, not perfectly, but persistently.

This book is more than a story. It's a reminder that no matter how broken life becomes, healing is possible.

And Sydney, this brave, beautiful soul, shows us the way.

Julie Fairhurst

Founder of Women Like Me

CHAPTER ONE

I n this small town, everybody knows one another, with most people being indigenous to one of the surrounding small islands, known as reservations. A place where it rains more than it shines, yet has gorgeous sunsets and beautiful scenery everywhere you look.

My dad, Darrin, and my mom, Alicia, broke up when I was just 3 years old. My dad left me with my mother to live a life of crime, drugs, and everything in between.

Both their moms, my granny and my grandma, are residential school survivors, where they endured physical, psychological, and sexual abuse as young children, which caused their kids and grandkids to experience intergenerational trauma.

This plays a big part in my story; my grandparents had no way to cope in a system that wanted our First Nations people to stay at the bottom. My grandparents persevered, yet their traumas ran through their veins just as fast as their blood did. It seeped into the pores of the generations after them. My parents didn't know any other way because their parents didn't either.

When I was four, my mom started dating my stepdad, Wilfred (Wil for short). We moved to Prince George, and on my 7th birthday and my mom's 27th birthday, my sister, Kymberlie, was born. I remember being upset that my mom missed my birthday, not realizing how random pregnancy and birth were.

Mom married my stepdad, Wil, when I was 8. Shortly after, we packed everything up and moved to Chilliwack, British Columbia, and I started Grade 4. We lived in Chilliwack for 4 years. My mom gave birth to my sister, Presley, when I was 11, and to my sister, Kennedy, when I was 13, both born in Chilliwack.

Side Note: My dad got a woman pregnant, and she gave birth to my brother, Texas, when I was 4 or 5, though I didn't meet him until I was 10 or 11, I believe. My dad was not around much when I was little. I was living far from Prince Rupert, where he was born. My stepmom, Kelly, gave birth to my sister, Kierra, when I was 11 years old. I believe I met her when I was 12 years old.

I have vivid memories of my mom and Wil drinking in the house with my sisters and me. Presley was still a baby.

The laughter that echoed through our home and the slurring of my mom's words always came before the screaming and arguing that pierced my ears, sending a chill down my spine. I always thought mom and Wil were fun when they drank because I had no supervision and could do whatever I wanted.

Sometimes they would go into our spare room, which had a lock on it, and would not come out all day. When they finally did come out, they looked like they had been awake for days. It was not often they did this, although they usually liked to drink in the kitchen.

It wasn't until I was older that I realized they were probably smoking drugs in that room; that was a horrifying realization, knowing there was only a door that stood between us and ingesting toxic fumes.

I would be responsible for looking after Kymberlie (4) and Presley (less than 6 months). I always wondered why they kept having kids. If I had to watch them all the time, I would have been 11! I barely remember how I did it; I assume it was with lots of cartoon watching.

I was the oldest, which put a lot of responsibility onto my shoulders. I had to take care of my sisters, or I would be in trouble, and if I refused, my mom would guilt-trip me until I changed my mind. I felt like I had no voice growing up, as if my thoughts and feelings didn't matter.

When I tried to express myself, my mom took it as disrespect; she always put soap in my mouth to "clean my words". I have a core memory of trying to tell my mom how she makes me feel, and she was fuming, unable to regulate her anger and overflowing like a boiling pot of water.

Instead of putting soap in my mouth, she made me drink a capful of laundry soap; I remember sobbing to her, begging her not to make me do this because I thought I would die. She shoved the cap in my hand, and it felt like a 100 pounds as I brought it to my mouth. The liquid burned as it went down my throat, piercing my taste buds while they screamed for me to stop. I felt the tears stream down my face as my mother watched me closely with no remorse; physically, I was fine, but in that moment, I had never felt so alone.

My mother's hands were never comforting. I knew if I wasn't ready, her hands could pierce my body like a weight; I would flinch if she raised them near me, especially if she was lecturing me over times when I just needed love. Her degrading tone and harsh names I was called have rang in my ears since the first time I heard them. Sometimes, I wish I could go back in time and hug my younger self.

She would talk badly about my biological dad, Darrin; I could not understand why she gave birth to me if my father was so bad. I felt helpless when she said mean things. If I said anything back, she would get so angry, which really frightened me. I would panic when she asked me questions I did not know the answer to. I was always scared of saying the wrong thing and getting hit. The littlest things would set her off; she would release her built-up rage and say she was doing it out of love, not knowing any other way to communicate with me.

A day before I started Grade 6, she slapped me with the back of her hand. It was unexpected; I had no time to prepare for the impact.

Immediately, I felt immense pain in my mouth and complete betrayal from someone who was supposed to take care of me. I had to tell people I fell on a doorknob so she would not get in trouble; however, my inner self was screaming and praying for someone to see through it and save me.

CHAPTER TWO

M y dad, Darrin, returned to my life when I was 11 years old. He was very inconsistent, in and out of jail, and that was challenging because sometimes I would not hear from him for months. He was constantly changing his number to avoid the police, and I thought it was to avoid me.

I felt like my dad forgot about me, like his world just kept spinning without his children in it. My dad, Darrin, had been selling drugs for all his life at that point. He would send me money because he thought it would make up for it, and my mom would take it right away to spend on whatever she'd like. Eventually, I would hide it from her and buy things I wanted that she would not notice.

At the beginning of grade eight, my mom and stepdad, Wil, decided that we would move to Terrace. I was 13, Kymberlie was six, Presley was 2, and Kennedy was a month old. It was an extremely tough time for me. I was in middle school in Chilliwack, and I had amazing friends that I did not want to leave, but I had no choice.

After we settled in Terrace, life took a turn.

My parents were drinking a lot; I saw them physically fighting on many different occasions. I would take my sisters into my room with me, away from the chaos. It was so scary but also so normal to me; they would break up after spewing vile words at one another, then they would get back together, and I thought that's just how relationships worked.

I started skipping classes, smoking weed, cigarettes, and drinking at 13 years old. I was caring less about school.

Mom and I were always fighting about something. I was rebelling and hanging out with the wrong crowd; I was internally screaming for someone to help me, yet I was met only with harsh words and raised fists.

I began to run away from home, often because I wasn't understood, I was criticized, and felt trapped, surrounded by walls that heard every terrible word ever said. When mom and stepdad Wil drank, it would always escalate.

I'd need to save my sisters from the people who were supposed to teach us kindness and respect; however, it was up to us to teach ourselves, while we endured war every day in our home.

Mom would say vile things to Wil, and, in return, he would physically hit her. They would be fighting in the living room, their bodies crashing into the couches and our dining room table; I would have to try to break it up or bring my sisters into my room because they would be scared and crying. It was tough having to comfort my three crying sisters while I was also crying and scared. I had to protect my sisters from my parents because I knew how it felt to be unprotected.

We moved to Prince Rupert shortly after I turned 14, and my teenage years got worse. I was fighting in school, skipping classes, and running away from home. One night, I was hanging out with three friends, and we decided to mess around in a building that was under construction. We trashed the place.

Then we broke into the video store beside it because my friend was able to break down the wall with a sledgehammer. I was 14 at the time and got my first criminal charge.

Shortly after, mom sent me to Chilliwack to live with my cousin, Chelsie, hoping things would get better. It did not; I was still doing the same things, just in a different city. One day, I was attacked by a girl who was mad that I beat her cousin up at school. After that, my mom made me move back to Prince Rupert with her a few days before I turned 15.

I lived with her for a couple of months before I moved in with my older brother and his wife in Prince Rupert.

Fun fact: I didn't know I had an older brother until I was 14, when I met him through my boyfriend, Greg, at the time. My dad found out around that time, too, but did not tell me.

Anyway, I was living with my brother and getting into all kinds of trouble. At 15, I was arrested with my boyfriend, Jordan, at the time, because he tried to bear mace someone, and I had the bear mace in my purse when the police found us. I was charged for possession of bear mace and possession of marijuana with intent to sell because, well, that is precisely what I was doing.

We ended up having a no-contact order, yet we could not stay away from each other. This caused me even more trouble and legal problems. We were charged (breached) multiple times for being seen hanging out together.

One day, there was this girl who caused grief to my friends, and I decided she needed to be taught a lesson. A friend and I went into her high school and beat her up very, very badly. I was arrested and spent four days in the adult city cells before I saw a Judge.

The judge ordered that I was not allowed in the City of Prince Rupert, I needed to live at my mother's residence in Port Edward (about 10 minutes out of town), couldn't consume drugs or alcohol, and I had a curfew of 10 pm. I had to check in with a probation officer every month in Prince Rupert with my mom.

I ended up getting arrested many times for breaching my conditions in the months and years that followed.

My mom and Wil were still always fighting or drinking; they would leave me with my sisters, sometimes with little to eat, and I did not really know how to cook.

I ended up moving in with my paternal grandmother in Prince Rupert, but I was on house arrest because I still was not allowed to roam Prince Rupert freely.

At 15, I would cautiously go out anyway. My grandma did not have many rules, nor did she understand most of my conditions, so it was easy for me. This led to more breaches and a longer period of probation. It felt like it would never end.

After five long months, I was finally allowed back in the city of Prince Rupert. I could walk around freely without fear of being seen by the police and arrested. By this time, the police officers knew me well.

Not even a month later, this girl and I were having some problems. I went into the mall area where she was, and I beat her up. I was arrested and put in the city jail cells. The next day, I saw a judge who ordered that I be denied entry to the downtown area of Prince Rupert. That is where my friends always were; it felt like I was banned from Prince Rupert all over again.

Two days after that, the same girl retaliated and beat me up! I was trying to avoid her because I was permitted to stay away from her. She was looking all over for me until she found me, and we fought. Cops heard about it, and I was almost arrested until I told them I was trying to avoid her, but she came to me and initiated it. The police wanted me to press charges, but I declined.

As much as it sucked getting beaten up, I did not want to stoop to her level and charge her like she did me. A few days later, that same girl and I had a mutual respect and became best friends.

CHAPTER THREE

As a part of my new conditions after that incident, I had to live at my mother's residence in Port Edward. I had a tough time staying at my mom's house because of the dysfunction and her intense rules, so I discreetly packed up my things and took a bus to Dawson Creek to stay with my biological dad, Darrin, who was on house arrest.

I had fun there! I had not had this kind of time with my dad before. He had a room ready for me and sent me with his friend to get whatever I wanted or needed for it. He was still selling drugs, so I witnessed a lot; I remember counting $10,000 in $20 bills for him while we sat and watched TV casually.

One night, my dad's friend and I were stopped by the police after we dropped off drugs, my palms were sweating as I frantically made up a name to give them when the cop shone a light in my face. I stopped breathing while they ran the name through their computer. I prayed they would let us go; when they let us go, I was finally able to take a breath. I stayed there for over a month before returning home because I missed my friends.

Additionally, I had not informed my probation officer of my departure, which resulted in several breaches that led to a warrant being issued for my arrest. I was hiding for a month or two after returning, then I was arrested.

They sent me to a juvenile center in Burnaby, BC. I was 16 years old; it was my first time on a plane, and I was handcuffed with a sheriff by my side. It was incredibly embarrassing. I was also afraid of being away from home and alone. I was not sure what to expect, but I remember making a friend there who helped me get through my brief week-long stay.

When I got out, I was put on a plane back to Prince Rupert and given conditions that were sure to set me up for failure. I was forced to live with my mom again, given an 8 pm curfew, no drugs or alcohol, not allowed in the downtown area of Prince Rupert, and I could not follow any of them. I continued to drink heavily; I could never stay home at my mom's because we did not know how to communicate with each other.

I was in toxic relationships with guys who were too old to be dating a teenager. I was easily manipulated and taken advantage of. I had low self-esteem because I had no idea what a healthy relationship looked like.

I thought it was completely normal to break up with someone and come back like nothing happened — no apologies, no acknowledgement of any wrongdoing, sweep it under the rug. I saw the red flags, yet I ignored them completely. I dated 19+ year old guys, and I thought I was special because they were putting themselves at risk by being with me. I had no idea that I was being groomed and taken advantage of.

As part of my conditions, I had to meet with a youth counselor every week for coffee. He really opened my eyes in many ways. He made me see these men for what they were, predators.

He lived an interesting life. He knew my father, Darrin, who used to hang around him and his criminal lifestyle. His teen and adult years were spent breaking the law, going to jail, and hanging with gang members until his late 30s or early 40s, when he got his arms and legs broken by a gang.

When that happened, he took a good look at his life and decided he wanted more out of it. He left that life behind and became a Youth counselor. He really made me feel like I had a chance to become something more, and I looked up to him very much, and I still do to this day.

CHAPTER FOUR

B y age 16, I had accumulated numerous charges and breaches, all of which were consolidated, and I had a scheduled sentencing date of June 25, 2013. I knew I would be going to jail, instead of facing my problems, I got scared and I ran away to live with my brother's wife in Prince George, BC.

My dad, Darrin, and my older brother were both in jail with each other at that point, in Prince George Regional Correctional Centre. My stepmom, Kelly, lived in Williams Lake, two hours from Prince George, with my 4 year old sister, Kierra, so I was also able to see them.

When my brother got out, I was happy to spend some time with him, but my dad was awaiting trial to see if he would be released or sent away for a long, long time.

Thankfully, he was released, and I was primarily living in Williams Lake with him, my stepmom, Kelly, and my little sister, Kierra. I was doing well there; I was not drinking or getting into trouble. I was spending time with my family and enjoying life again. I wanted so badly to stay, but I knew that eventually I would have to go back to Prince Rupert and face my criminal charges that I had run away from.

My dad, stepmom, sister, and I drove to Prince Rupert with the intention of me turning myself in. I decided to drink and hang out with my friends instead. I did not want to lose my freedom because I was afraid of not knowing how long I would be gone.

I was hiding at my friend's in Prince Rupert for about a week. In early September of 2013, I was outside my grandma's house when I saw a police car coming down the street. My dad and little sister, Kierra, were outside, and I ran inside to hide.

The police officer saw me and pulled over to question my dad. He told them that I was not inside, but my 4 year old sister let them know I was very much inside and corrected my dad when he, again, tried to say that I was not. So, I had to come out and face the consequences, but now my sister jokes that she "ratted" me out.

The police officer arrested me and left me in a jail cell for two days before I saw a Judge. It was cold, quiet, and boring. I was given microwaved waffles and Subway sandwiches that had everything I did not like on them. I did not eat much.

When I saw the Judge, it was a man who had previously sentenced me many times. He knew I had not learned from my mistakes, so he sentenced me to 30 days in the same juvenile detention center I was in last time.

One day later, I was escorted by a sheriff through airport security, and it felt like all eyes were on me. I felt like a failure in that moment, wishing I had dealt with my criminal charges sooner. I hopped on a plane with the sheriff, flew for 2 hours to Vancouver, BC, and then we had to drive 30 minutes to reach the detention center — my new home for 30 days.

I had to strip my clothes while they searched me to make sure that I did not have any contraband, then they gave me new grey sweatpants and a grey shirt. I settled into my small jail cell, looked at the four walls, the window that had bars on it, and my bed that was stiff and uncomfortable; I had a brief cry before I went out to meet the other girls who were there.

There was a group of girls in my unit who were not as friendly as the ones I had last time. They had no manners, they would glare at me, and they were cold and unwilling to be my friend.

One girl was there for murdering someone, and I made a mental note to stay away from that bunch. They would taunt the girls who were quiet or shy, or they would loudly talk about them so they could hear. I was sick of it, but I knew if I stood up to them, three or more girls would jump me. I bit my tongue, and it was extremely hard to hold the anger and hurt I felt inside of me.

I was moved to a separate, smaller unit that had about six other girls, and it felt a lot easier than dealing with the 12 girls in the other unit. I got along with most of the girls very well. I shared a lot of interests with them, and a lot of them grew up with dysfunctional parents or foster parents who were not pleasant. Some of the stories I would hear humbled me very much because they had it worse than I; traumas at an early age were common in that group of girls.

The days felt so long. I spent a lot of time reading, focusing on schoolwork we were able to do while we were there, and playing games with the other girls in my unit. I had a good relationship with most of them, except this one girl who always got on my nerves. I managed to ignore her for most of my sentences. Four days before I was released, she challenged me, and before even thinking, I started hitting her. I did not stop until the guards came in and threw me in my room.

Shortly after making sure that the girl was okay, they took me to a unit with absolutely no one in it and stuck me in a cell with nothing but a book and a blanket. For the next three days, I was only allowed out of my jail cell for an hour.

In that hour, I showered, called my mom briefly, and changed my book before heading back to my cell. I felt so stupid for letting my anger get the best of me; instead of ignoring the girl, I hurt her physically and emotionally. I had no idea if I would be arrested as soon as I was released, but it was another charge added to my record.

For 3 days, I sat with my thoughts and really realized I wanted more for myself. I had no idea how I would do it, but I felt like the life I was living was not for me. When I was released from jail, thankfully, I was not arrested for the assault charge; it was something I did not need to deal with for now. A sheriff drove me to the airport and ensured I boarded the plane safely.

I made it home and was happy to sleep in my bedroom. I was grateful to have a room there still. I checked in with my probation officer, and he told me he had found a room for me at a youth treatment center. I was reluctant to go, but if I didn't, I would have to go back to jail.

So, five days after being released from jail, I had to say goodbye to my family and friends again. It was very emotional; I did not want to leave them, and I had no idea what to expect. I felt like I did not have a problem with drugs or alcohol so that it would be a waste of time.

CHAPTER FIVE

I flew back to Vancouver with my probation officer and met with a woman from the treatment center. I said goodbye to my probation officer and went with the woman to the treatment center in Chilliwack. When we arrived, it was not what I had expected.

It was just a house on a street on the outskirts of Chilliwack. It looked so normal that I thought we were at the wrong place.

Once inside, it looked empty. There were a few pictures on the unwelcoming gray walls, the air was stale, and it seemed like nothing was out of place.

There was only one other girl living there, so I had the option to choose between three different rooms, and I selected the one downstairs. I unpacked my things and stayed in my room for the rest of the day to set it up how I liked.

On November 11th, 2013, I spent my 17th birthday in treatment. The workers got me gifts, cake, balloons, and took me to the movie theatres to make my day special. I could not be more grateful for it. I was missing my family, but the workers and the other girl there made me feel special on my birthday, regardless.

I had to spend 5 months in treatment; during my time, we worked on something called a 16-step program. Being there and doing the program helped me with all my anger, gave me a safe space to talk about my traumas and my feelings, while also keeping me out of trouble.

I finished most of my schooling and was working on getting my driver's license. I really enjoyed my time there and thought that I would love to pursue a career in this field once I am older.

At one point, my past caught up with me, and I had to go to court for my assault charge from jail. The Judge threatened to send me back to jail until they saw how well I was doing in treatment. Eventually, the charges were dropped.

After five months, I had to say goodbye to everyone in treatment and went back home to Prince Rupert. I was feeling confident and ready to face the world head-on. I did not realize how hard it would be to stay sober once I was back home. I was only sober for a week before I started drinking again. I had a fun night, but felt like a failure the next day.

For the next month, I drank with friends and avoided going home. I got into a fight in public with a girl who was picking on my cousin/best friend, Taylor. The police officers were called, and I went back into hiding.

I had to take hidden trails when I wanted to get somewhere. It felt like my heart stopped when the police drove by, but I kept my head down, hood up, and acted as normal as I could.

That went on for a month before I was finally caught and arrested. The judge sentenced me to 21 days in the Burnaby detention center, where I was before.

This time, things were more settled, and the girls were less hostile. I had a good relationship with most of them; I kept my composure when girls would get heated because I did not want any more charges.

I was 17, turning 18 that year, and I knew I did not want an adult criminal record. So, after 21 days, I was released and sent back on a plane to Prince Rupert. The next day was sometime in June, and it was an exciting day for me because it meant I no longer had a 10 pm curfew! It was important for me mainly because that was the reason for most of my charges, aside from assaulting people.

I spent that summer drinking profusely and doing various drugs every other day. I was always drunk and high, doing whatever I could get my hands on. This went on for two long months with no end in sight.

I was spending time with a 32-year-old man and a couple of other friends, but that man supplied me with drugs, or I would get money somehow to get my own drugs. I didn't like hanging out with that guy to begin with because my mom had always warned me about him, and my dad said he would hurt him very badly if we ever spent time together.

He was known to hang out with teenage girls and even sexually assaulted one of them. I always made sure to keep my guard up around him, but he never gave me any problems; probably because he knew my dad, Darrin, was a scary guy.

Thankfully, in August, my mom, my sisters Kymberlie, Presley, and Kennedy, were going on vacation to Kelowna, BC, and brought me along. I went through minor drug withdrawals. The drive there was the worst, 15 hours in the car, and I had to hide how sick I felt; otherwise, my mom would know.

We met Wil in Kelowna, who was there for work, and spent over a week doing fun things. We were at the beach daily. I tried parasailing with my sister, Kymberlie, and we even went on a giant inflatable obstacle course that was set up on a lake. I had an incredible time there, and we made lots of memories.

Eventually, we returned home to Prince Rupert, and I did my best to stay away from drugs and the people who did them. It was a lot easier not to do drugs than it was not to drink alcohol. I continued to get drunk with my friends every other day, but I managed not to get reckless and break the law.

In November, two months later, I turned 18! I was both happy and afraid. My probation officer informed me that if I did not incur any additional charges for 3 years, my juvenile record would be expunged, meaning it would be erased. However, if I did get charged with a crime after 18, my juvenile record would follow me for the rest of my life.

By then, I was aware that it would severely limit me in life, and I did not want that for myself. At this point, I would drink, but I was no longer the girl who picked fights with people, and I was content with that.

CHAPTER SIX

By December of 2014, I started hanging out with a guy named Shane. He liked to drink a lot, and that is how we started hanging out. I was attracted to him almost immediately; he was handsome, could always make me laugh, and made me feel safe whenever I was with him.

At first, he was reluctant to date me because he knew he was an alcoholic, but I did not care because I was one too, and I thought we could help each other. On Christmas of that same year, he asked me to be his girlfriend. I felt like I was on cloud nine because he made me so happy. We made each other happy.

We were always telling jokes or playing pranks on each other; we loved making each other laugh. He was my best friend, and I knew I could talk to him about anything without any judgment, and he could do the same.

We spent every moment we could together; we'd walk around our small town, day or night. He'd tell me stories of his time fishing, mushroom picking in the bush in the next town over, and he enjoyed skiing and would go every year with his dad, Rob. They both shared a love for the outdoors, something I hadn't really experienced before.

As time went by, drinking together became hard. Shane had a lot of jealousy from past relationships that were projected onto me. He would get jealous of the male friends I had — true friendships I had to let go of — because I thought that was normal in relationships. I never gave him a reason not to trust me, but he had been cheated on many times in the past, and he was afraid I was doing the same.

After a few months of being together, we broke up. I was feeling hurt because I wasn't cheating on him, but he had a hard time trusting me. After a few days of discussing our feelings with one another, we got back together. Things started getting better for our relation-ship, and he was finally trusting me a little more every day.

Shane's dad, Rob, had worked at the Prince Rupert Port Authority (the port for short) for decades; the only way you could get a job there was if you were given an applica-tion from someone who already worked there.

Every year, the Port would distribute one application to the union workers, who could then give it to someone they deemed suitable. When Rob got an application, he gave it to his youngest child, Shane, right away.

Shane was ecstatic. This meant a lot to him because it was an excellent job to have; he always admired his dad's career and work ethic, and he wanted to follow in his footsteps. Plus, it paid very well. Once accepted, he began his training, which took a month to complete. This really helped Shane stay away from alcohol, and our love grew stronger as I supported him fully.

While Shane completed his training, I signed up for a course that would help me get multiple certificates. I was in the course for six weeks, and I learned so much. I received approximately 15 different certificates, including First Aid and Traffic Control Person (TCP); these were the main reasons I wanted to join. My stepmom, Kelly, was a TCP, and it was familiar to me.

Life just seemed like it was finally coming together for not only me, but Shane and me as a couple. We had each other; we were both working towards a better life together, one that wouldn't revolve around partying all the time.

We would meet up whenever we had a chance, which wasn't often because of my course and his work schedule. Our love grew so strong within four months of dating, and we were both growing in so many ways. I wasn't getting into trouble anymore; I had calmed down and was no longer constantly breaking the law. Shane's life no longer revolved around drinking and endless parties; he had stability, discipline, and his depression seemed to be slowly leaving his life.

Once his training was done and I had finished my course, life became dull again. It was difficult for me to find a job in Prince Rupert, but Shane could not move away because of his career. While his job at the port paid well, it was inconsistent.

Every morning, he had to wake up around 7 AM and go to the dispatch center to see if he had work that day. The supervisors would call names in alphabetical order; if it reached your name and you were there, you'd have a job. If you weren't there and it called your name, you'd lose out on $350+ that day; you would have to wait for the list to go all through the alphabet and reach your name again.

Shane was incredibly determined to make it every day, though. Sometimes he would work every other day, and at other times he wouldn't work at all because business was slow.

When it was slow, Shane and I would drink a lot, and when we drank, we would fight over pointless things. He would insinuate that I was cheating, or I would freak out on him for not trusting me. Sometimes I would say I'm going to cheat on him, so he would have something not to trust me for; obviously, that would escalate the situation instead of solving it. The next day, we would apologize and move on as if it didn't happen.

One day, my breasts were hurting, and I immediately thought, "I'm pregnant!" I told Shane, and we walked downtown to the mall to pick up two pregnancy tests. Then we went to the washroom separately and agreed to meet back outside.

After peeing on the sticks, I washed my hands and went outside to wait for Shane. He still wasn't outside, but the tests confirmed that I was pregnant, and it felt like I was waiting an eternity for Shane to come outside.

I felt so uneasy, I thought the wind would scoop me off my feet. I couldn't believe I was growing a little human inside of me. When Shane came outside and I told him he had the biggest smile I had ever seen him wear, his eyes lit up like the 4th of July. He gave me a warm hug and kissed me so fiercely.

We were going to be parents! I was in shock, with little words to say, while Shane's face was beaming with pride as he looked at me with a twinkle in his eye.

I texted my mom, my stepdad, Wil, and dad, Darrin, because I was afraid of what they would say. They were, without hesitation, so excited and happy for us and for their new roles as grandparents! It was my mom and step-dad's first grandbaby, and my dad's third grandbaby.

When Shane told his mom and dad, they were beaming with pride that their youngest baby was having a baby of his own. Our unborn child was already so loved by its grandparents, aunties, and uncles. Shane and I both had four sisters and two brothers each, though he lost his sister, Eva Dawn, ten years prior. Shane's mom gave me a huge hug, and our families welcomed each other with open arms.

CHAPTER SEVEN

W e both knew that we needed to make changes in our lives. At that point, we were living with his mom and not in a financially stable position to move out on our own. We had only been dating for six months, and neither of us could take care of ourselves.

I was terrified of having a baby; Shane was always drinking, and we argued a lot. I was terrified of raising our baby alone, but I knew it was a possibility if we did not figure out our relationship.

We ended up moving in with Shane's older sister, Sandy, so we could save money to afford our own place before our child was born.

Around this time, Shane's dad, Rob, found out he had cancer in his neck. He was sent to Prince George for more testing. Shane and his siblings were very worried for him; they feared the unknown.

It was an extremely challenging time for Shane; his dad was his best friend, and he didn't want to lose him. His dad wanted to fight, so he was doing chemotherapy regularly, some in Prince Rupert but mostly in Vancouver. He was always driving to Vancouver; he enjoyed his drives there, which took about 2 days to complete.

Shane would go out and drink a lot, then he would come home, either angry or happy; there was no in-between. I had no idea how he would be after a night of drinking. We would spend a lot of time arguing about whether he wanted to drink. I would shut down after exhausting conversations about how I didn't want to live in this constant emotional state, and break up with him, thinking that might stop him from drinking and be present for my pregnancy, but it never did.

He would drink for a few days, then he would apologize, and we would end up back together. The further along in my pregnancy I got, the more hormonal I would get. I would say mean things to Shane if he wanted to drink, which made him drink anyway. It was extremely hard crying to myself, knowing my baby could feel every intense emotion. I couldn't really talk to people because they would tell me to leave him. I couldn't do that, though, because I felt like our child needed both parents.

It wasn't always bad, though; most of our fights were only because of his alcoholism. Shane would make me feel like the most beautiful girl in the world, even if I felt bloated and huge from pregnancy. He would rub my feet if they were sore and run me a nice, warm bath with my favorite chocolates on the side. He loved buying me gifts and took me on dates weekly; he always spoiled me.

In October, we went to the doctor who wrote the sex of our baby on a folded piece of paper, and I gave it to my mom without looking at it. We wanted a fun little gender reveal, so my mom put pink or blue paint into squirt bottles, then wrapped grey tape around them to hide the color.

Shane and I had white shirts on, blindfolds over our eyes, and we were given the bottles. We started trying to squirt the paint on each other as much as we could before the bottles were empty. I remember hearing Shane say that I got it in his mouth, and I couldn't stop laughing. It was so much fun and a moment I will always treasure.

Once we took the blindfolds off, we looked at each other, and we were covered in blue paint. We were having a boy! We were so ecstatic, he couldn't wait to teach him how to fish, ski, and do everything he did with his dad growing up.

By the end of October, we finally found a two-bedroom apartment and moved in. We rented out the second room to his sister, Michelle, though she rarely stayed there. Everything felt like it was falling into place. Shane was working more; we were slowly but surely getting every-thing we needed for our baby boy.

At the beginning of January, Shane went out drinking and was ignoring me the entire time. He didn't tell me where he was or what he was even doing, just radio silence. I remember there were poker chips and cards on the table when I came home, so I threw them all onto the ground in anger, then packed up my stuff and left.

We had broken up and were arguing so much via text before I blocked him, so he couldn't contact me. Somehow, he ended up getting a hold of me and sent a goodbye message that he'll always love me, but he couldn't take his depression anymore.

He sent me a picture of his slit wrist with blood every-where; I was horrified by what I had seen. I was frantic, looking all over for him, calling people to ask if they had seen him, and when they said they hadn't, I feared that he was dead.

I was crying uncontrollably, I couldn't catch a breath, nor could I even make out words to express the way I was feel-ing. Once I was able to move, I drove to the hospital, and I found him. He was in a hospital bed with a bloody gauze over his wrist: as soon as he saw me, he covered his red, swollen eyes with tears in his face.

I could tell he was drunk, and he just kept repeating that he didn't want to see me right now. I was very relieved he was alive, yet deeply hurt by the events that had just unfolded; my eyes were burning, and my heart was broken. I left the hospital crying. I had no idea how my body could cry for hours yet still have enough fluid for more tears to fall; I was eight months pregnant.

He ended up cutting his wrist so deeply that he needed to have surgery to stitch his tendons; otherwise, he would have had no use of his thumb. He had to wear a cast for six weeks.

After this incident, Shane made the decision to quit drinking and fully be there for our son and me. Later, he told me that when he cut himself, he thought of me and our baby, and he ran to the hospital without hesitation.

When Shane quit drinking, things became so much better. He was present, loving, emotionally attuned to himself, and eager to meet our son soon. We were no longer arguing all the time. We got a little Pomeranian from my mom, and we named him "Biggie" because he was so tiny and fluffy.

Shane's dad, Rob, gave us a 2007 red Dodge Magnum, and we were so thankful! I had my license, but Shane didn't, so I drove it. We would take drives to Port Edward or the next town over, give our friends rides, and we just loved driving aimlessly together.

On February 19th, 2016, Shane was outside smoking, and I woke up around 9:30 AM to use the washroom. Afterwards, I went back to my room, and as I was about to lie down, I felt something wet going down my leg. I went outside to tell Shane my water broke, and he said, "Are you sure it wasn't just pee?" I told him I had just gone to the bathroom — it was my water breaking!

Shane started panicking and called his male cousin to let him know my water broke. His cousin was panicking with him, and his cousin's wife said, "Give me the damn phone!" before telling Shane to calm down and get ready to head to the hospital.

I wasn't feeling any contractions at that time, so I was casually taking a shower before leaving because I wasn't sure the next time I would have one.

We got into our car and headed to the hospital; I called my mom to tell her to meet us there. The nurse checked and told me I was 3CM dilated, so they were admitting me. Around 11 AM, my contractions started, and I would walk around because that was the only thing that gave me some comfort. I would be in the shower with hot water running over my back while Shane fed me strawberries. I absolutely did not want an epidural because I heard stories of them messing up your back, though at one point, I got fentanyl. After all, the contractions hurt so much.

By 3:30 PM, I was ready to start pushing. I had my mom and Shane in the room helping me through it. My mom was watching the birth, and Shane was beside me while I clutched his arm in pain. I was screaming and crying, wondering how women could want more than one child after feeling this pain. I was mad at Shane for being a useless man and not having to go through this feeling like my body was going to give out on me at any moment. I deeply regretted not getting an epidural and wondered why I couldn't just have one now. I just wanted to change my mind and leave the baby in me. Looking back on it makes me laugh at my dramatic thoughts.

After pushing for what felt like forever, at 4:11 PM, my son was born; hearing his first cry echo throughout the room was as beautiful as hearing sound for the first time. He was placed on my chest, his little body, his head full of dark hair that looked just like his daddy's, his deep brown eyes were adjusting to the hospital lights but completely mirrored his daddy's eyes, and his little hands reaching for mine made me forget all the pain I had just gone through.

He was remarkably perfect. He had my button nose but looked like Shane in every other aspect. He weighed 10 pounds, 4 ounces, and was barely fitting newborn diapers. We named him Kayden Robert Hunter Gaudry, his daddy's last name, and his middle name was Shane's dad's name, who was still aggressively fighting cancer.

I remember looking at Shane's arm, which I was holding onto during labor, and it was covered in bruises from my tight grip. I had no idea I was holding onto it so fiercely.

Two days later, we were able to bring Kayden home. I was

so sore and weak, I felt like a zombie walking out of the hospital, moving slowly as if I was going to fall apart.

We brought him home, and our parents were always coming over to see their grandson. For the next month, Shane would work while I stayed home to take care of our son. Shane would still help me with him at night, even if he had work in the morning. Sometimes when I'd wake up with our son, our dog would wake up and hang out with me while I fed Kayden.

In March, Shane wanted to go near the Skeena River to catch Eulachons, little fish that are popular among indigenous people, representing the first fresh food source after the long winter.

While Shane fished, I hung out with Kayden in the car because it was too cold for him outside. We had such a good day, though, regardless. Shane was happy to fish, and he caught so many Eulachons that he kept just enough for us and distributed the rest to family who couldn't get them themselves, a wholesome gesture of giving back.

Later that day, I really wanted to go to a bar and have a drink. I was pregnant for my 19th birthday, so I didn't get to experience bars yet. Shane and I talked about it; we told each other this was a one-time thing, and we wouldn't make a habit out of it because Shane was 58 days sober at this point.

So, we dropped our son off at my mom's house and headed to the bar. We had a good night with friends and especially with each other. Most of the night was spent talking about our son and our love for him.

We ended up drinking a few more times before breaking up yet again. I moved all of mine and Kayden's things to my dad, Darrin's, house to stay with them. One night, I decided it wasn't fair to move out so Shane could drink in our home. My dad and I went to the apartment while my stepmom, Kelly, watched Kayden.

I was banging on the door while my dad went around back and literally climbed up onto the balcony of our second-floor apartment and got in, scaring the crap out of Shane and his friends. Shortly after, Shane and his friends left, and then my dad left, knowing the cops were coming and he would get arrested if he stayed.

Once the cops got there, I told them I was the one causing a disturbance because I wanted Shane out of the apartment we shared. They looked around to make sure it was just me, and I let them know my son was safe with his grandparents before they left.

I sat in the empty apartment trying to tidy up when I found an unopened bottle of liquor that Shane had left behind. I went over to a friend's house, drank the bottle, then went home and drank some more. I drank for two days straight before I sobered up and went to get Kayden from his grandma.

I was texting Shane when he came home so that we could work things out. Our parents weren't impressed with us, and my dad was especially upset with me for taking Shane back. I hated the loneliness and didn't want to raise our son by myself, so Shane and I worked it out before making the decision to quit drinking together.

Once we got sober, life started to get better again. We were enjoying our little family and watching our baby learn new things every day. Kayden enjoyed tummy time, and our puppy loved snuggling with him. We would go to the waterfront to take photos together. We loved to drive everywhere with Kayden and Biggie, and Kayden would always fall asleep in the car.

CHAPTER EIGHT

A pril 24th, 2016, was one of the most traumatic experiences I've ever encountered throughout my life.

I remember the day so perfectly; it was a surprisingly sunny day in the usually rainy town of Prince Rupert. I woke up in my home with my beautiful family, the one I created with my son's father, Shane. He was asleep on our bed while I was playing with our 2-month-old son and our dog, Biggie.

My son's grandma, Sylvia, wanted to take him for the day, so we drove to his grandma's to drop him off, and I told my baby I'd see him soon. We usually would take our dog everywhere with us, but that day, for some reason, we decided to leave him home.

Shane and I decided that we'd take advantage of the beautiful day and drive to the lake. We picked Shane's cousin up before we went on the highway to the lake, which was about 15 minutes out of town.

Shane wanted to drive, but there was nowhere to pull over; therefore, we'd have to wait to switch spots at the Oliver Lake rest stop 5 minutes out of town.

We were listening to music when I noticed a blue car coming out of nowhere, and I saw it swerve in my rearview mirror. I knew they had to be drunk because they were driving so recklessly on the one-lane highway.

My heart began to race, my palms were sweating, and I gripped the steering wheel so hard that my hands were throbbing. I was so afraid that I couldn't find my voice to tell Shane that the people behind us were drunk.

We were just around the corner from Oliver Lake when the blue car swerved into the other lane to pass me. When I thought they were passing me, I felt relieved. I began to slow my vehicle down to let them pass, but they ended up losing control of their vehicle and collided with the driver's side of my car.

My car flipped a few times before coming to its final resting place, facing the opposite direction we had been driving.

When we came to, Shane asked us if we were okay, but I was unsure. He couldn't see me, so he climbed out of the car through his window, and he was immediately horrified by the seriousness of the crash.

When we rolled, the roof on my side was crushed; I was stuck between the windshield and the crushed hood of my car, unable to move. My head was bleeding profusely, and Shane was literally looking at my skull. When I tried to move my legs but couldn't, I knew immediately that I was paralyzed.

The adrenaline was pumping through me, so I didn't quite understand the severity of it all. I remember my neck felt extremely uncomfortable, and I tried to push my head out. I was unsuccessful and completely trapped. Shane was hysterical, saying that he couldn't believe that this was happening.

The four people in the other car jumped out, and one of them climbed onto my car's hood to ask if everyone was okay. When he jumped on my car, I felt an extreme amount of pressure in my neck, and Shane told him to get away from us because he was hurting me, and I could tell right away that those people were drunk.

A paramedic who was off duty at the time witnessed the entire crash unfold and came to help. He assured me that help was on the way, though it felt like ages before they arrived.

I remember repeatedly asking them just to call my mom so I could talk to her one last time. It was music to my ears when I heard the sirens. I felt relieved knowing that I'd be in good hands soon.

When the paramedics analyzed the situation, they realized that the roof of the car would need to come off to get me out safely. We needed to wait for the firefighters to get there because they needed to use the jaws of life to take the roof off for me to be safely removed from the windshield.

I remember how loud and terrifying it sounded when they were cutting the metal that trapped me.

After being trapped for over an hour, they got the roof off, and I was free. I fell back slowly while about 5 or 6 people kept my neck and head steady. In one swift yet gracious move, they laid me down on the stretcher.

I remember looking up at the beautiful, blue, cloudless sky while they carried me out of the ditch. I blacked out shortly after getting into the ambulance.

I was air lifted from Prince Rupert to Vancouver General Hospital (VGH) by helicopter, although the only thing I remember is asking where Shane was and throwing up in the helicopter before blacking out again.

Once I was at VGH, they gave me an MRI to get a clear understanding of my injuries. My spine was fractured in multiple areas; C7 and T6 were completely shattered with bone fragments going into my back and spinal cord area, C7 spinal cord was pinched, leaving only about 3mm left,

C6 was fractured, T1-5 and seven had major swelling, and a slight hemorrhage near the spinal cord.

My scalp was 'degloved' and left open for nearly a day; Prince Rupert Hospital did nothing to prevent infection. My right wrist was basically twisted, then pushed towards my hand, completely shattering it, and it was pretty obvious when looking at it.

I had a partially collapsed right lung, but was still breathing on my own at that point. To top it off, I also had a blood clot in my right carotid artery.

The next day, the first surgery was to clean and close my scalp, which was 8 inches. It started from my right eyebrow, going to the middle of my hairline, before going into a C shape, with 5 inches hidden in my hair, and ending near my right ear.

On April 27th, 3 days after the crash, they did surgery on my spine to put screws and metal plates in the C7 and T6 areas and remove bone fragments. Lastly, they put a metal plate and screws in my right wrist and successfully removed the blood clot in my right carotid artery.

I was breathing on my own until I went into acute respiratory failure post-op. On April 27th. I had to be put on life support and was in a coma for 5 days in the Intensive Care Unit (ICU). I ended up with sepsis for 8 days, and they couldn't figure out why. I had intense hyperthermia, and I always had ice packs or a cooling blanket on me to keep my temperature down.

After 6 days, they found the cause; basically, it was pneumonia in my bloodstream, which is often fatal. Among that, they also found that my head was bleeding and possibly infected from being open for so long. They packed the small opening on my head with gauze that would stay in there, and nurses were required to cut 2CM of the gauze out of my head every day. It took a month to pull all the gauze out. It felt like salt being poured on my wound each time it was pulled, but the very last day, they pulled out 15 cm, which was excruciatingly painful.

Once I woke up from a coma, I remember my cousin, Natasha, telling me that I was in a car accident, and I was thinking, "Wow, that was so long ago, why are people still talking about it?" because I didn't understand where I was or the severity of my injuries.

I was heavily medicated and hallucinating to the point where I was 100% sure that the nurses in VGH were trying to steal my lung to give it to their relative. It felt like I was running all over the Lower Mainland trying to get away from them, but they kept finding me. I would try to tell my family members when they'd come to see me; however, they couldn't understand me due to the breathing tube down my throat.

It was so surreal; it still feels like it happened, even though I know it was a hallucination.

I remember conversations I shouldn't have, and I even spent time with my dad, Darrin's father, who died when I was 3 years old. I remember being in my room when a nurse told me that I was getting into a wheelchair because I had a visitor. I thought it was odd that they couldn't come to see me in my room like everyone else.

The pain in my neck was extremely sore, but they pushed me into a small waiting area that was empty except for one man in a wheelchair with his back facing me, and he was watching the TV. I had an intense sensation come over me that I just knew it was my grandfather, my dad's dad. I was so afraid to look, so we sat and watched TV together while we had a conversation that I wish I could remember.

I was afraid that if I looked at him, I'd have to go to heaven too, but everything in me knew who that man was. A couple of years later, my mom spoke with a medium; my dad's dad came to her and told her that he was with me during the car crash. He explained that he couldn't stop it from happening, but he wrapped himself around me like a cocoon, saving my life. He ensured that I would still have use of my arms/hands, and he did because if my injury were any higher in my neck, I wouldn't have finger function and would have minimal arm function. After hearing that, I knew that my grandfather had come to see me while I was still in a coma.

I had to stay in the Intensive Care Unit (ICU) for nearly a month.

During that time, I couldn't hug or kiss my son; he couldn't visit much because I had an infection, and everyone who came into my room needed to wear PPE. I spent my first Mother's Day in the ICU; thankfully, Shane and my parents brought him to see me briefly.

On May 15th, 2016, I was moved out of the ICU and onto the Spinal Unit on the 9th floor in VGH. I was groggy during my time in the ICU due to excessive pain medicines, but when I moved to the Spinal Unit, that's when I started working aggressively to get better and transition into this new life.

I would do "breathing trials," which were when I would be taken off the ventilator and needed to breathe on my own for a period of time, each time being longer than before. It absolutely exhausted my energy because it was hard after not being able to breathe on my own for so long. I remember when I would breathe on my own for an hour, and it felt like I sprinted through a marathon. This went on for a few months; I couldn't swallow anything and could only communicate by typing or writing.

After seven weeks of being in the hospital, the cast on my wrist was able to come off, the doctors cleared me to put pressure on it, and that's when my physiotherapy began. I needed to learn to do everything over again, so my son and I shared many milestones together.

We learned to sit up around the same time. I remember during one physio session, Kayden and I were holding each other up and balancing gracefully. After 3 months of not eating or talking, I was able to breathe on my own and only needed the ventilator while I slept. My son and I shared a honeydew melon when I was finally able to eat.

In July, I was transferred to G.F. Strong Rehabilitation Centre, a place where they would help me transition into my new life with a C7 spinal cord injury. They helped me regain about 65% of the movement in my hands. They taught me the necessities for everyday life, things that were once so easy became hard to overcome. Just trying to use my fingers and thumb to grab something was frustrating.

CHAPTER NINE

Around the time I got to G.F. Strong, Shane and I were having problems. He was travelling to Prince Rupert to work, and when he was there, he would drink every other day, miss work, and have suicidal thoughts.

When I was still in VGH, his brother was staying with him and introduced him to Heroin when Shane was still in a vulnerable state. I had no idea until I got to GF Strong and was more mobile and could contact him more.

When I found out, I freaked out and broke up with him. I knew that I couldn't handle his addictions AND work on getting better physically, mentally, and emotionally... So, I had to let Shane go. It was incredibly hard; I didn't know how I was going to get through my new life without his support.

I didn't know how I would care for my 6-month-old son without his dad. Ultimately, I called Shane's dad, Rob, who got him a bus ticket to Prince Rupert and away from heroin.

By November 22nd, 2016, I was discharged from GF Strong and moved to Surrey with my mom, my dad Wilfred, my three sisters, and my son. I lived with them for 2 years while they did what they could to make this new life easier for me. I lived downstairs in the basement suite with Kymberlie and Kayden while my mom, Wil, Presley, and Kennedy lived upstairs.

It was hard adjusting to my new life. There were many days, weeks, months where I felt like I couldn't go on, like I'd be better off dead. I was filled with anger; I despised the people who ignorantly drank and drove, taking away the future that I had planned before being permanently stuck in a wheelchair. I had my independence taken from me; I never thought I'd get it back; I thought I would have to live with my parents for the rest of my life.

I was adamant that I didn't want to drive ever again; I figured I'd use transit or rely on others to drive me. That lasted about 10 months before I reached out to start Drivers Rehab and learned to drive with hand controls.

On May 25th, 2017, I drove for the first time. It felt amazing. From then on, I completed 10 sessions of Driver's Rehab and was officially able to drive on my own. I had a

2016 red Dodge Grand Caravan that was fully accessible and equipped with hand controls so I could drive.

Slowly but surely, I was regaining some independence.

My next goal was to find a house of my own. Living with my family again was hard. There was a lot of yelling and arguing, I didn't want my son growing up around it, I couldn't handle my mom and me butting heads all the time.

My dad, Darrin, lived close, so I was at their house a lot. I'd use my manual chair, and my dad would literally pack me up the stairs to get me inside. I was looking every day for 2-3 bedroom houses for Kymberlie, Kayden, and me. It was so discouraging when I'd ask if a place was wheelchair accessible, they would say it was, just for me to get there, and they would tell me, "It's only a few steps to walk up."

This kept happening over and over again; I felt defeated. One day, I viewed a home that was wheelchair-accessible. It was a tiny two-bedroom house, but I agreed to a year-long lease then and there. 3 days later, I moved into the suite with Kymberlie(14), Kayden(2) and I (21) in March of 2018.

Shane and I were talking on the phone a lot. He was struggling financially, was about to be evicted from the apartment we once shared, and he was partying too much. I convinced him to come to stay with us and be present to watch our son grow. He immediately agreed, and I got him a plane ticket on March 27th, 2018, the day before his 28th birthday.

I was so happy to have Shane here with us, to witness him bond with Kayden, to see him finally get away from the drinking and drugs his life revolved around since the car crash.

You see, when Shane went back to Prince Rupert after we broke up, he quit heroin but started smoking crack. He still lived in the apartment we once shared, but he refused to sleep in our room; instead, he rented it out to friends who also smoked crack, and Shane slept in the living room because it was too painful to sleep in our room.

He was extremely depressed; he didn't go on social media for 2 years and just had a landline that I would call him on. He was hurting so badly, he felt like he failed us, and he couldn't forgive himself for leaving, which sent him into a downward spiral. I was busy with my own hurt and couldn't be there to help him with his. So, when we finally had him down here with us, I was so happy for him.

At first, Shane and I were basically living together and co-parenting, but after about a week, we had a huge heart-to-heart one night and got back together. Those were some of the best times of my life, our family was pieced back together, and Kayden had his dad back in his life!

Shane wasn't drinking as often, he altogether quit drugs, and we were all happier than we've ever been. Kayden was learning things I couldn't teach him, and he had someone to play with on the playground. I was limited in playing in parks because of either the play structure or the wood chips around the park. Shane had no problem chasing our boy anywhere and everywhere. We'd go to indoor jungle structures, and Shane and Kayden would have a blast! It was heartwarming to see them bonding with one another.

The first few months were amazing. Shane and I were falling in love with each other all over again, putting our broken pieces back together, and feeling stronger than ever. I was learning to love life again, becoming more confident in a wheelchair, and Shane was always telling me how beautiful I am. We would go out to drink occasionally, and we always had a good time, making random friends along the way, and Shane would always tell them our story of how we overcame everything that stood between us.

Of course, it didn't last. Shane would travel to Prince Rupert for work, and when he was there, he would drink excessively and accuse me of cheating, or we'd get in an argument about something else. I was constantly scared of him not coming back and Kayden losing his dad again.

There were times when Shane would get drunk and choke himself until he was about to black out, then he'd stop. It wasn't to necessarily kill himself; he just wanted to feel some pain, I guess. I was always terrified that one day he'd be too drunk to stop himself and die.

I'd lie awake at night crying silently to myself because I didn't know what to do about Shane. It was hard to deal with Shane's depression while also dealing with my own. I was still trying to cope with being paralyzed by a drunk driver. It took them 2 years to finally charge the woman who was driving drunk, and every day before that felt like the judicial system failed me.

As a teenager, I got charged for way less, and it just didn't seem right to me. This woman altered my life and my family's. I would never walk again because of this woman's reckless decision. I was furious with all 4 of the people in the car that day, and I had no idea how to stop being mad.

CHAPTER TEN

On June 15th, 2018, Meagan (the drunk driver who hit me) pleaded guilty to Impaired Driving Causing Bodily Harm; therefore, we got a sentencing date for November 2018.

She ended up becoming addicted to heroin and living on the streets of the Downtown East Side in Vancouver. She was severely addicted to drugs, which unfortunately came before her kids, family, and our court proceedings. She missed many court dates, but they kept letting her out shortly after arresting her; it was infuriating. I hated her for not only changing my life but also skipping court appearances, which was a slap in the face.

Not to mention absolutely hating the justice system for completely failing me every time they would let her out.

By late December 2018, Shane and I had broken up for good. He was drinking too much, and I had emotionally checked out of the relationship. I loved Shane when he was sober, but I couldn't stand him when he drank.

He flew back to Prince Rupert and found a place with his sister, Michelle.

His dad, Rob, ended up staying with them for end-of-life care. The cancer doctors had no more life-saving treatments to try with him, and Rob ultimately died on January 29th, 2019. This absolutely crushed Shane. He turned his phone off and partied for 3 days straight, drugs and all. I was so worried about him; it wasn't unusual for him to turn his phone off and party, but it was usually only a day or two at most. I was messaging his friends until I found Shane, and they reassured me he was alive.

I flew to Prince Rupert to be there for Shane as well as his mom and sister, Sandy, with whom I was very close. I did my best to be there for Shane, but I ended up drinking and doing cocaine with him and his friends while I was there.

This was very out of character for me. I recall when I was doing it with Shane, and he said he didn't like this version of me; I didn't either. I flew home and got back into my routine.

I would text Shane to ask him about Kayden. I would ask when he's going to visit him, whether he'll make it to

Kayden's 3rd birthday on February 19th, and if he could send some money to help me out — things like that.

By then, Shane was annoyed with me and would lash out at me for not thinking about his feelings. He had lost his dad, his biggest supporter in life, and his days were spent partying to cope with his grief. My perspective on it was very different, though.

Shane had checked out of fatherhood yet again and left me to be a single mom. At this point, Kymberlie had moved out, and it was just me and my 3-year-old. I was the one who cleaned, cooked, and cared for Kayden. I would deal with his tantrums, his fussing, his three-year-old behavior, all of it while Shane was partying. It would be heartbreaking to hear my son cry because he missed his daddy; he didn't understand why his dad wasn't around anymore.

It felt like because Shane lost his dad, Kayden also lost his. It was infuriating, but luckily, I was able to bring Kayden to my mom's house or my dad's house when I needed a break.

Shane and I completely cut communication for months. I was on dating apps, seeing other men, trying to keep my mind occupied while missing Shane, being angry with him, or angry with Megan for constantly missing court dates.

When Megan missed her sentencing on April 26th, 2019, my two best friends, Taylor and Emily, and I went to the

Downtown Eastside to look for her in person. Unfortunately, we didn't find her, and I went home feeling completely defeated.

I had shared a Facebook post about her disappearance that went viral, and a woman from Victim Services in Prince Rupert contacted me on April 28th. She told me that she remembered the day of my accident, the only highway to and from Prince Rupert was closed, she was amongst the pile of cars waiting, and the police told her I was a new mom. She shed many tears and even prayed for me that day.

She sympathized with my situation and informed me that she was hosting a luncheon for victims and survivors of crime and would be honored to have me attend it in Prince Rupert on May 28TH. She couldn't pay for my flights, but could accommodate me in a hotel for two nights. I was honored and immediately agreed to it.

By May 3rd, Megan had been arrested and released within a day with a "promise to appear" for sentencing on June 7th. I couldn't believe they wouldn't hold her until then, after she failed to show up for every other sentencing date. The justice system was completely failing me.

Around this time, I reached out to Shane. He informed me that he was a bit more stable, not partying as much, working more, and wanted me to bring Kayden when I went to Prince Rupert for the luncheon. We concluded that I would leave him there until I came back for sentencing on June 7th, then Kayden would fly home with me. It seemed fine because Shane's mom, Sylvia, was more than happy to watch her grandson when Shane was at work or needed a sitter.

Shane and I began communicating more about Kayden, and it really seemed like things were on the mend. Shane and I weren't being so hateful towards one another; he was Facetiming with Kayden and me regularly, sent some money to help pay for our tickets, and it just seemed like we would be able to co-parent in a healthy way. We had even planned on attending a music festival together, either in Vancouver or somewhere in British Columbia.

On May 27th, Kayden and I took a plane to Prince Rupert; it was Kayden's first plane ride! Shane and Sylvia were the first to greet us, and we went to my hotel room. We had a nice chat before they took Kayden and left to do their own thing. I met up with one of my best friends, Patricia, and we decided to go to the bar to drink, where we met Shane's sister, Sandy. I always called Sandy my sister, and she always called me hers. We had so much love for one another.

We enjoyed our night at the bar and stayed until 2 AM before I went back to my hotel to sleep. The next day, I attended the luncheon for survivors and victims of crime; it was amazing! I felt so honored to be invited to this luncheon, and I was also mentioned/recognized during it.

It was a blessing after feeling defeated by the justice system.

After lunch, I went to take a nap in my hotel. I woke up around the time Shane got off work, and he told me he was taking Kayden to the docks to fish. I thought that would be fun, so I decided to go with them. Kayden was having a blast learning to fish; he was his dad's little shadow, copying everything his dad did. I got a lot of photos of them bonding, and I was so happy that my son had his dad again.

Afterwards, Shane wanted to drink, and I wanted to as well, so we decided to have some drinks together while our son slept at his grandma's. We planned to meet some friends at the bar to hang out. Shane and I were still kind of warming up to each other again after basically hating each other for months.

That night we had an amazing time. We were joking around all night, just like we used to; we had dark humor that few understood, but we did. We caught up on our lives and worked on the things we were still mad at each other for. We laid everything out bare and forgave one another. I ended up getting so drunk that he physically drove my chair back to my room, and we fell asleep together.

The next day, I packed my things and said my goodbyes to Kayden and Shane, gave them big hugs, and Shane told me he'd see me soon. I wanted to tell him I love him, but I got scared and decided not to. I got on the plane and headed back home. That night, Shane took Kayden camping with his friend, Justin, and Justin's son, Hunter. Kayden had a blast making s'mores, looking for small crabs that were under rocks by the water, and Shane was giving me updates along the way. He couldn't stop telling me how happy he was to share these moments with his best friend and their sons.

CHAPTER ELEVEN

On June 1st, the prosecutor who would be sentencing emailed me to say they couldn't reach Meagan to confirm her travel arrangements for sentencing in Prince Rupert on the 7th. A warrant was put out for her arrest.

He told me that if they couldn't find her by the 3rd in Vancouver, there wouldn't be enough time to arrest her and transport her to Prince Rupert by the 7th. Of course, they didn't find her, so sentencing was postponed yet again, to August 30th, 2019.

I let Shane know, and he said he would take a flight with Kayden to Vancouver to bring him home around the 12th once he had the funds.

While Kayden was in Prince Rupert, my childhood friend, Tre, was living in Surrey, and we were drinking almost every day. We would drink a bottle of Absolute Vodka and a case of beer every other day.

When I was sober, I'd communicate with Shane and Kayden while they gave me updates on their time together. Shane was spoiling Kayden with whatever toy he wanted; he would drop Kayden off at his mom's in the mornings, then head to work for the day. Afterwards, they would do something, but there were a couple of times where Shane would drink, and Kayden would spend the night at his grandma's.

I wanted to express how I thought it wasn't right, but I couldn't say much considering how much I was drinking with Tre. I remember telling Shane how much I was drinking because I didn't know what else to do without our son. Shane laughed and said, "See! You hypocrite!" before laughing away.

Side note: Shane had broken his phone when I went to Prince Rupert, and I told him I could get him a new phone on my phone plan as long as he paid for it. His last phone was on my phone plan, which he paid for, so it wasn't an issue for me. He agreed, and I ordered him the newest Samsung; he received it on June 7th.

On June 8th, Shane brought Kayden to his mom's in the morning and then went to work as usual. There was a Sea Fest parade in Prince Rupert that day, and Shane was sad he had to work and couldn't enjoy it with Kayden. He was sending me videos and communicating with me throughout his day at work.

Around 6 PM, he facetimed me, and I answered. The camera was facing the ceiling, and I saw strobe lights, a dimly lit room, and colors all over. I immediately knew he was at the bar. He joked with me that he was hanging out at home, not doing anything. I laughed and said he must be a stripper in training if his home looked like that.

We had a good facetime call. He told me he was having a few beers and going home. Kayden was safe at his grandma's for the night. We talked and laughed for a bit longer before we hung up.

That night, I decided to stay home and catch up on sleep. Just after 10 PM, out of the blue, Shane sent me a message saying, "You hurt me," and another he quickly deleted before I could see it.

I saw the message 2 minutes later and messaged back asking, "How so?" Then it was just radio silence; he wouldn't elaborate on why he thought I hurt him and where that was coming from. I figured he was just drunk and thinking of something from our past because this wasn't the first time he'd gotten mad at me when he got drunk.

I tried to call him, but he didn't answer, so I let it go, thinking, "I'll ask him about it when he's sober."

The next day, I couldn't get a hold of Sylvia, and Shane wasn't answering me when I asked about Kayden. Sylvia was hard to get a hold of (usually because she rarely answered her phone) and I figured Shane was binge drinking, which was why his phone was off.

I was getting anxious that I couldn't get a hold of Shane or Kayden, and by the end of the day, I had a combination of being scared that something had happened to Shane and mad that he could leave me in the dark if he were just binge drinking.

I started messaging some of his friends asking if he was with them before I fell asleep that night.

By the morning of June 10th, I woke up to some of his friends' messages back letting me know they hadn't heard from him since the night of June 8th. I felt the color drain from my face and an immediate pit in my stomach because I just knew something was wrong.

I called Prince Rupert Police around 9 AM to request a wellness check for Shane. I gave them his home address, and they told me they would go check things out. I messaged Shane's best friend, Justin, and told him what I knew. He said he would ask around to see if anyone had seen him. I called Shane's mom, Sylvia, who finally answered; she updated me on Kayden and said she hadn't heard from Shane in a couple of days. I messaged Tre, and he was the only one I told my exact thoughts to.

I said, "I'm freaking out because I think Shane is dead." He told me to calm down, that that's probably not the case, and that he's out binge drinking somewhere.

An hour went by, and the police called me. They said they couldn't get in because the door was locked, and no one was home. I told them to break down the door and force their way inside, but they said they legally can't. I was so upset with them because wellness checks are exactly when you should be able to do whatever it takes to get inside.

Justin was looking at the spots where Shane frequently hung out. He went to his dad's house, but Shane wasn't there. I looked at Shane's Samsung cloud, and his last known location was at Shane's home. I told Justin he should try to break in because I think he's there.

By this time, I was at my best friend, Taylor's, house because I just couldn't be alone. I was an absolute mess. Taylor's mom lived like a minute from Shane's house, so she was asking her if she'd seen or heard from him, but she hadn't.

Justin let me know that he got into Shane's house, but he wasn't there. I felt slightly relieved. However, Shane's bedroom door was locked, and Justin couldn't access it. Unbeknownst to me, Justin remembered a time when Shane locked himself out of his room and had somehow opened it with a butter knife. I found this out later.

Around 2:30 PM, Taylor and I were in her living room when she got a call from her mom. She went to her room to take the call. I followed behind her in case it was about Shane. I stayed in the hall to listen in. Her mom said that there were ambulances, police, and firetrucks at Shane's house, and Sylvia was on the ground crying, but I just heard Taylor say "WHAT?! ARE YOU SERIOUS?! Sydney's at my house, Mom!"

I went into her room and said, "What? Is it Shane?! Taylor! Turn around and say something!" with tears in my eyes. Taylor turned around, crying, then just nodded, and I completely broke down. I just let out a huge cry, the kind where there's no noise and you don't even breathe. I didn't take a breath for two minutes. Then I started sobbing, and I couldn't stop. I was screaming "NOOO!" and crying without breathing.

I just wanted to unbuckle my seatbelt, fall to the floor, and curl into a ball. I was leaning completely forward, crying the hardest I've ever cried in my entire life, and I kept feeling like I couldn't breathe. Taylor was crying and kept trying to get me to sit up, but I just couldn't. I didn't want to believe Shane was dead, so I told Taylor to phone her mom back to confirm that he was for sure gone.

Unfortunately, it was true, and Shane had hung himself.

I was so numb, I couldn't believe that Shane was gone, just like that. I couldn't wrap my head around how someone could just be here one minute and gone the next. I thought about the last thing he messaged me, and it felt like it was all my fault. I would never know what I did so wrong to hurt him.

I wished that I had tried harder to contact him that night. I called him once that night, but beat myself up for not calling him consecutively until he answered. I was going through wave after wave of emotion right in Taylor's hallway; it was the absolute worst day of my life.

I went outside once I wasn't crying hysterically. I just sat outside and smoked like four cigarettes while Taylor called my mom and stepdad, Wil, to tell them the news. I was in no shape to drive, so they came to drive my van for me. I called my dad, who didn't answer at first, so I called my stepmom, Kelly, to let her know that Shane passed away, and she called my dad to tell him. They came to Taylors, and we met outside before heading to my house.

My mom and I made a plan to drive to Prince Rupert in the morning with my auntie Vicki, who could help my mom drive because I was in no shape to drive at all, let alone for 17+ hours. Once we got to my house, there was family in my living room, and I just went to lie in my room feeling completely defeated.

My dad, Darrin, packed my suitcase while I just lay in bed, watching videos Shane had sent me the previous day. I would go in between crying hysterically and feeling like I was in a trance, wishing I could wake up from this nightmare. It was pure hell, mainly because I was so far away from my son, who had just lost his daddy.

The next day, we left at 4 AM and picked my auntie Vicki up in Chilliwack. That entire drive was horrible; I was listening to Shane's favorite Linkin Park album on repeat, and at times, I would cry so hard they'd have to stop the car and get out to remind me to breathe. I don't remember much else from that drive.

We pulled into Prince Rupert around 2 AM and immediately went to pick up Kayden from a relative's house. I was so happy to finally see my hyper boy! We checked into our hotel, and it happened to be the same room Shane, Kayden, and I stayed in the year before. It was crushing, but I was exhausted and just glad I was here with Kayden. I pushed past the feeling of dread, and I just tried to embrace the good memories we shared in it.

The days that followed were hazy. I went to visit his mom and siblings, and it felt good to see them all. We cried, we laughed at some memories, and I felt closer to Shane being with them all. It seemed like some blamed me for his death, but I just brushed it off, thinking it was in my head.

It was much later that I found out people did, in fact, blame me for his death, but that's not until later in the story. I went to see Justin, his best friend, and he told me what happened that day when he found Shane. I can still picture it to this day, and I have immense guilt because I called Justin and asked him to look for him.

On June 19th, I received a call from the prosecutor that Megan had been arrested. I honestly didn't care; they told me she would be in jail until sentencing on August 30th, and I still didn't care. I had bigger things to worry about, like how I was going to get through Shane's memorial that very same day.

I got to the place where they held his memorial. A friend of mine was on her way out and told me it was an open-casket memorial. I had not prepared myself for that at all. When I got inside, I broke down in tears and quickly went outside. My aunties and mom were with me, telling me to find the strength to go in or I would regret it. I was very hesitant, but ultimately my auntie Bonnie called me and was the one who convinced me by saying, "Babe, this is the hardest thing you're going to have to do, but you NEED to go in. You come from a long line of strong women, and you CAN DO THIS!"

I wiped my tears, took a deep breath, and went inside. I found a spot next to my cousins, aunties, and mom; sitting in the front beside Shane's open casket were his mom, his three sisters, Sandy, Michelle, Shannon, and his brother, Mike.

Shane was in his casket, and off to the side were six of his greatest friends he'd ever had, the ones who were carrying his casket. I could see in each of their faces how unmistakably heavy this was for them, not the weight of his body and the casket, but the fact that they never thought they would be pallbearers for their 29-year-old friend, Shane.

I couldn't handle it; seeing how hurt everyone was, seeing the side of Shane's face, his lips I once kissed, his nose, his hands I've held many times before, it was all too much for me.

I left abruptly and told my family that I would be right back. My cousin asked if I wanted company, but I said I would be okay, just going to get some air. That was a lie. I left quickly and started roaming around town trying to get away before anyone could see me. I listened to Shane's favorite song, "One More Light" by Linkin Park, with my headphones in while I smoked cigarettes and cried with my shades on.

Everywhere I went, I had a memory with Shane; sometimes I would laugh, and sometimes I would cry, thinking about it.

Ultimately, I decided to go to the casino, where Shane and I loved having a drink. I went out onto the balcony, which overlooked the ocean, and the sunset was just beginning, painting the sky a beautiful pinky-orange. I asked the waiter for a Budweiser, Shane's favorite beer. I wasn't much of a beer drinker because it was gross to me, but I did it for Shane.

I drank the Budweiser and wrote letters to Shane in my notebook, telling him everything I wish I had said when he was alive. I was there for the entire memorial, about 2- 3 hours; I knew in my heart that this was the best way for me to say goodbye to Shane, not at the memorial, feeling like I was going to throw up.

People told me I would regret not saying goodbye at the memorial, but to this day, I don't. My "memorial" to him was having his favorite beer at one of our favorite places, where we shared so many good memories together.

Shane was cremated, so there wasn't a formal funeral where we met at the cemetery to bury him. Instead, the next day, Shane's family held a feast and gave gifts to those who helped him in some way, shape, or form. Many gifts were given away, along with cash donations, to express thanks in traditional ways. Later, we ate food that was made and brought by different families, basically a potluck or smorgasbord.

On June 22nd, my mom, Kayden, and I said our goodbyes and drove back home to Surrey. I felt relieved to be going because it was too hard being in Prince Rupert, where, everywhere I looked, I had a memory of Shane. The drive home was heavy, but it was easier because we had my 3-year-old to make us laugh and keep things light. I figured it would be a lot easier once I'm home. I'd miss my aunties, uncles, and cousins, but I was excited to see my dad's step-mom, my four little sisters, and my best friends Taylor, Emily, and Tre.

Emily and Tre cleaned my house for me while I was gone, so it felt so lovely to come home and not have to clean. I felt like I had gotten closer to my mom than ever; she supported me and held me up during those days, and I was so grateful for her.

Kayden and I dropped my mom off at her house in Surrey, then we drove to our home in North Delta, near my dad Darrin's. It was eerily quiet, and it made me realize we hadn't really been alone at all in the last 12 days. Being alone with my thoughts was absolutely the worst. I was barely able to care for Kayden. I was miserable, not taking care of myself, staying in bed with Kayden to watch movies; my will to live was very minimal.

Kayden spent a lot of time at his grandparents', either my mom's or my dad's, and I was being quite selfish about it. I hung out with Tre a lot, and when we hung out, we'd drink and cry. I got a tattoo for Shane above my heart. I'd write to him every day. I felt like I couldn't talk to anyone, and no one wanted to talk to me.

My dad was there for me, and we'd go there frequently so Kayden could run around or play in the pool. If Kayden slept there, I would pick Tre up and drink to have a friend to talk to. Emily and Taylor seemed uncomfortable when I brought up Shane; they ignored me and took a step back.

CHAPTER TWELVE

O n July 3rd, it was a tough day for me. I was missing Shane so much! I felt so alone. I just wanted to escape it all. I messaged Tre to ask if he wanted to drink; he was reluctant at first because I expressed how sad I was feeling, and he said, "It's probably not a good idea if we drink then."

Tre was an alcoholic, so it was easy for me to convince him it would be fine, just like the other times. I dropped Kayden off at my dad's house and immediately went to pick Tre up. We went to the liquor store and picked up a bottle of Absolute Vodka with a 24-pack of beer around 3 PM.

We were drinking all day, we were laughing, crying, blasting music, and drinking on an empty stomach; a horrible combination mixed with missing Shane and wanting to be with him. It's all a blur, but around 9 PM, I remember saying that I was getting tired and might go to bed. The next thing I remember was something I'll never forget.

I came to with a piercing pain in my left shoulder. I had no idea what was going on. I looked around, and I was in the middle of my van, where my chair locks in. I see Tre trying to wake me up through the shattered window on the left side. I couldn't wrap my head around what was happening. How did I get here? Where am I? Why am I in my van? Why is my arm hurting so badly?

I was screaming in pain and trying to gather my thoughts. What happened was far worse than I imagined. I was in another car accident, was it my fault? I thought surely it must have been someone else driving; it wasn't Tre, he wouldn't do that.

Unfortunately, it was Tre who was driving. I guess during my blackout, Tre brought up driving, so we got into my van and went for a drive. Tre got into the driver's seat, and I stayed in my chair and locked it in the middle part of my van where it usually goes. Tre and I ended up missing our turn and going onto the highway over the Alex Fraser Bridge near Surrey/North Delta; Tre drove us all the way to Richmond and took a turn off on NO. 6 road to try to head back home. He ran a red light, and we got T-boned on the driver's side, which is why my left shoulder was in so much pain.

The van got hit and was redirected to an open field on the right, where it stayed. I was stuck in the van because my ramp wouldn't come down for me to get out; therefore, the paramedics had to pull me out of the broken window.

My collarbone was fractured, but by the grace of God, everyone was alive. Tre was arrested for a breach in his conditions as well as drinking and driving; I was brought to a hospital still inebriated and not fully understanding what had just happened. I called Taylor, then my dad, to let them know what happened; he immediately started crying.

I was given IV fluids and slept for a few hours. When I woke up, I couldn't believe it wasn't just a nightmare; it was reality. I didn't have my wheelchair, my shoulder was killing me, I was in a hospital bed with no way home, and my phone was dead. I was sitting in a hospital bed crying because I couldn't believe that I put so many people in danger, I felt betrayed by Tre for driving my van, and I felt disgusted in myself for being in the van with him.

Although I don't remember ever agreeing to it, I know that I must have because I was in the van too. I felt horrible for the couple in the other vehicle; how scared they must have been, how they got hurt because of our reckless actions. We put so many lives in danger from the long distance we had gone; it's a miracle that we didn't get into a crash on the highway in the 18 kilometers we had gone. I was physically sick to my stomach over it, and I still am to this day.

The couple in the other vehicle had whiplash and were bruised, but they were otherwise okay physically. I later found out the woman was traumatized; it was hard for her to get in a vehicle and drive for a while, a feeling I knew too well.

While I was still in the hospital, I borrowed someone's phone charger to plug mine in. Once it had enough battery, I had to call the yard my van was towed to for them to try to get my power wheelchair out of the van.

This took about an hour. Then I called a cab to pick up my chair and bring it to the hospital, and a nurse met the driver outside to retrieve it and bring it to my bedside. I was given the okay to go home. I had to use a lift to get into my chair because I could not slide myself with a broken collarbone. Even using a lift was hard because the sling would squish me and make my shoulder extremely uncomfortable.

Once in my chair, I had to use my right hand to control the chair on the left side of me; that was going to take some time to adjust to. I went outside, looked at the name of the hospital, and that's when I realized I was in Richmond. I had to call a taxi, and luckily, the hospital social worker gave me a taxi voucher to cover my fare home.

When I got home, my TV was still blasting music, and my house was a complete disaster. There were empty beer cans and liquor bottles in my living room, as well as some uneaten fast food from the night before. I tried to tidy my house while I sobbed in pain, physically and mentally, at everything that I had just gone through.

I had no van, my collarbone was broken, and I was immobile. I was in a car crash because of my and Tre's reckless decisions. I lost my friend Tre, and I felt such fierce anger towards him for putting me through this.

My dad came to my house that night; he instantly gave me a big hug, and we both just sobbed. It was so heartbreaking. He helped me into bed, which is where I stayed for a couple of weeks. My dad stayed with me for that entire time he cared for Kayden; he brought me anything I needed, cooked, cleaned, etc.

I had to adapt to this new reality that I only had one working limb, my right arm. I learned to transfer with one arm and had to adjust to using my right hand, even though I'm left-handed. Everything was physically demanding, not to mention the mental effort of sorting out my thoughts. I quit drinking for nine months, and I cut contact with Tre.

Everyone was incredibly upset with me, my moms, and my dads; ultimately, they were glad that I was alive, though. Emily and Taylor stopped talking to me and started talking about me, laughing and judging my grief. It was such a dark and disturbing time for me; I wouldn't have made it out alive if it weren't for each of my parents, siblings, and, of course, my son.

In mid-August, my power chair suddenly lost all power. I had no idea why, and when someone came to look at it, he determined it was fried, and it would need to go into the shop for a month or longer.

I was left with only my manual chair, something I didn't use often because I would get exhausted quickly during short distances. My collarbone wasn't healing appropriately because of how much I needed to use my arms, and being in a manual wheelchair would severely delay the healing process, but I had no choice.

I was also left with a difficult decision regarding court; I would either have to attend Meagan's sentencing and read my victim impact statement by video in Surrey or push through the struggles and read it in person at the Prince Rupert Courthouse.

It would be a big challenge, getting to the airport, flying to Prince Rupert, and getting around the uneven town with an abundance of hills, all while my shoulder was hurting every time I pushed myself. I gave it some thought and decided it would be best to show the judge in person just how hard life is for me because of Meagan's actions. I wanted to look her in the eyes while I read my victim impact statement to her and the judge.

A few days before we were scheduled to leave, her lawyer reached out to inform us that Meagan was refusing to appear in person and would attend by video court. She was lashing out in jail, hurting herself, and acting rather crazy in her cell. Her lawyer said it was "quite childish", but her reasoning was that "her back hurt and she didn't want to ride in the sheriff's van all the way to Prince Rupert".

I was so upset because I literally had pain in numerous parts of my body, yet I was going to make it to sentencing in person. They couldn't force her to, so she was allowed to attend by video from jail. I hated her more than anything in that moment.

At the time, I didn't understand that she was probably just ashamed to show her face and come to terms with the damage she had caused me.

Well, we flew to Prince Rupert on August 29th, and it was tough to get around in a manual. Luckily, I had a lot of friends and family to help push me from A to B. The next morning, Shane's sister, Shannon, pushed me to the courthouse for the sentencing.

I rolled into the courtroom with the amazing support of my friends and family, and I was ready to leave this chapter in my life, even though I hated Meagan so much and wasn't about to change my mind.

When I was in the courtroom, I read my Victim Impact Statement without shedding a tear. I did not want to cry in front of that woman, and I did not want to mess up my important words.

After hearing what she had to say, we took a lunch break. I turned to the prosecutor and burst into tears because I wanted to tell her something that I never thought I could ever say or do. My friends and family thought I was crying because of my victim impact statement; they came to hug me right away. I didn't tell them the real reason I was crying.

We came back after lunch, and I was very emotional when I told her these words. I said, "I forgive you; I forgive you for everything you've done and caused. I hope one day you're able to forgive yourself. My son didn't lose his mommy, so your sons shouldn't lose theirs. I hope you embrace the tools in jail to get sober and clean, and I hope one day you can repair the broken bond with your sons."

Everyone was shocked. I had been carrying around this burden, this baggage that was never mine to carry. I gave it back to her and felt immediately freed from the hate and anger I felt for her.

The Judge sentenced her to 18 months, but with time served and serving only 2/3 of her sentence, she was released almost 8 months later. Everyone was upset that her sentence was so short, but I reassured them there was no reason to be upset because I feel so free and ready to close this chapter in my life. For her to get any jail time was good enough for me, plus it meant she had a chance to get sober and maybe get her kids back in her life.

She got out in April 2020 and shortly after, went back to using heroin. I was disappointed but continued to move forward in my life. She died of a drug overdose in February 2023; her body wasn't found for over a week. I was distraught for her sons, who lost their mom; however, I was quietly happy that she wouldn't ever be able to hurt another person again.

After the court was over in 2019, I went home and tried to heal from everything I'd been through, from losing Shane to being the cause of a car accident to having Meagan finally sentenced. It all really weighed on me once I was home, and I fell into a deep depression.

I could no longer cope with alcohol; I had to feel everything completely sober, which was HARD. I didn't have any friends because grief was too uncomfortable for them. Taylor was saying bad things about me and treating me like crap. Emily called CPS on me, saying I was drinking with my kid around me, false claims because we disagreed.

Rumors were going around in Prince Rupert saying that I told Shane to kill himself that night; Shane's sisters hated me, Shannon threatened to kill me, Sandy refused to give me back Shane's new phone, and I had to pay $2000 because it was in my name. When she finally gave it back over a year later, I got excited thinking I could give it to Kayden to look at his photos and whatnot on it.

Everything was wiped from the phone; to my surprise, all his photos were gone, and I was crushed. Shane was very photogenic; he took videos and pictures constantly, and it absolutely broke me. So many people turned their backs on me; I didn't fully understand how much grief changes people. I was starting to believe that it was my fault for Shane's death, I was questioning all our fights and how I wished we could have worked it out between us, but we didn't know how.

I was isolated from everyone I thought would never turn their back on me. In October 2019, I was ready to commit suicide and was extremely close; it was all planned out, so no one close to me would find my body.

At the last moment, I thought about how my son would lose both his parents to suicide, and I told my mom. She immediately got me in contact with a therapist, and I started to build myself again from the ground up.

My therapist, Rebecca, helped me come to terms with everything that had happened in my life. I had to unlearn a lot of toxic traits that I didn't even know were toxic. She would remind me that I had helped Shane on numerous occasions when he was feeling suicidal, that he had lots of unresolved traumas, and the way he left wasn't my fault.

She gave me a safe space to talk about my feelings and helped me work through them all healthily. I still practice those tools daily and am incredibly grateful for her. I found a way to forgive myself for the things in my life that were never my fault to begin with.

I knew that I needed to do the hard work to stop the intergenerational trauma that ran through many generations on all sides of my and Shane's families. My son was only three years old when he lost his dad; he could not afford to lose his mom, too. Kayden will always be the reason I push myself to do better. If it weren't for him, I would have thrown in the towel and given up in 2016.

I started drinking again around the time Meagan got out of jail in April/May of 2020. I'm not quite sure if it had to do with her or the pandemic that drove me to drink again. I ended up getting into cocaine and was immediately hooked. I struggled with cocaine and alcohol from 2020 to 2022 because I was dealing with a lot of stressful situations and was no longer in regular contact with my therapist.

I never did it in front of Kayden, though. I made sure he was safe with his grandparents. We always had what we needed, which is why I didn't think drinking and snorting cocaine was a big deal; it was only once a week, it's not like I was out doing heroin. That was my reasoning, terrible, I know.

In August 2022, I quit drinking and quit cocaine. I didn't drink for 15 months, then I drank excessively for a bit when my sister, Kymberlie, moved in with me. As of 2025, I rarely drink; on special occasions, I might, but I stay away from drugs and have since I quit in 2022.

I bought a van in September of 2020; however, I was adamant that red Dodge vehicles were my worst enemy. This time, I purchased a grey Toyota Sienna and am much more responsible with it. I hide my car keys if I drink, and I continue to call the cops on anyone who drinks and drives.

I bought a three-bedroom house in 2021; it is everything I dreamed it would be. It's easy to get around in my power chair. I have a roll-in shower in the bathroom in my room, a big yard for my son to play, a nice neighborhood on a dead-end street, and my son's school is very close.

He is such a thoughtful, kind, rambunctious, hilarious, and happy kid that I'm incredibly proud of. He's growing so much, and I feel like I've grown with him. I was young when I had him. I was still growing and learning how to take care of my baby while living in survival mode.

Kayden is the reason that I'm also striving to be a better person, woman, and mother. It took years to realize that I wasn't living, I was just surviving and waiting for another traumatic event to happen to me.

I'm very independent now compared to how dependent I was in 2016 after my accident. I cook, clean, take care of my son, our house, and our two cats, Mac and Garfield, and I can drive myself around.

In 2016, I was so afraid that I'd need to live with family for the rest of my life, I never thought I'd be able to thrive independently, yet here I am, killing it every day.

My moms and my dads are such active grandparents, my dads are great role models for Kayden and teach him things that I can't as a single mom who is wheelchair bound.

Wil brings Kayden fishing; they are constantly building something in their garage; my mom and Wil always want to bring him out for walks and to soak up the beautiful scenery this world has to offer. My dad, Darrin, taught Kayden to ride a bike and to swim; they are always outside.

I have a lot of health issues that come with a spinal cord injury. I am prone to Urinary tract infections (UTI), so I'm in and out of the hospital frequently. When I need to go, my dad always drops everything to look after Kayden and often stays with me when I need it.

In July 2024, I drove to Prince Rupert for a wedding, and on the drive back, I was feeling physically horrible; once I got home, my mom took Kayden, and I went to the hospital. I was experiencing sepsis due to an untreated UTI and was in the hospital for seven days.

Because of my spinal cord injury, I can't pinpoint where the pain is coming from; I'll get intense spasms in my legs, stomach, and back area that make it hard to do anything. My blood pressure will rise, and my heart rate will slow, making it feel like a pounding in my chest. I'll get intense migraines that make it feel like someone is squeezing my head. If it gets too bad, I will cry from the pain and not be able to think about anything for 5-10 minutes until the pounding stops.

In July 2025, I had to drive to Prince Rupert for my aunt's funeral. On the way home, my sister had a cough that was starting. By the time we were home, I had developed a cough, and it worsened the next day. My injury is above my lungs, which makes my lungs not have the same capacity they had before. Because of this, I can't cough and get phlegm out easily.

I tried to sleep it off, thinking that it would help. My dad came to take care of me while Kayden was at my mom's. By 10 PM, it was increasingly hard to breathe. I was freezing so much that my teeth were rattling, and I was shaking. I could not get a good breath and called 911.

They took me to the hospital, and I found out I was VERY septic; I was diagnosed with Pneumonia, given inhalers, two different IV antibiotics, and was in a hospital bed for six days, on oxygen that entire time. It was a terrifying experience, but it made me much more aware of germs and how regular illnesses can affect me more severely.

Before my car accident, I had a good, strong immune system and had never stayed in the hospital or needed surgery. After my accident, I had nine surgeries, 100's of

ER visits, too many scars to count, and a terrible immune system.

CHAPTER THIRTEEN

W hile writing this book, I was getting used to a new manual chair; I have always used powered chairs, but I wanted to regain some arm strength, which is why I purchased the manual chair. It would slide while I was trying to transfer in and out of it, which made me uneasy.

As a result, I fell out of my chair twice in the first 9 days. The way I fell the second time caused me to have neuropathic pain throughout my body that felt like a jolt of lightning. After that, my legs would shake at random times, which made my body stiff and my back tight. My head felt compressed with a constant migraine, taking my energy, and it would get worse if my foot were touched, and there was visible bruising on top of it.

At first, I didn't think much about it until the next night, when I had a good look at my foot and saw it had bruised significantly; I knew there was something broken almost immediately.

The next day, I went to the emergency room to get an X-ray; the doctor told me he couldn't see any visible breaks, but a radiologist could read them better, though they were backed up. The night after, I got a call from the radiologist who let me know he had seen "some fractures" and wanted to get a CT scan of my foot for a clearer image.

I got a CT scan the very next day, which showed I had broken my big toe, the two toes beside it, and there was an old fracture on my pinky toe from an unknown time. It took 5 days to confirm my suspicion that I had broken my toes, and the orthopedic doctor advised me to wear a sturdy shoe for the time being.

I'm worried about the healing process simply because I won't know if it's healing correctly, and if it's not, I might need surgery to correct it. Only time will tell...

I'm terrified of dating anyone and letting them into my life because I feel that's too big a risk to make. I made the mistake of dating a man in 2021, whom I fell for too easily, and let him around my son too soon. His name is Jordan.

We had chemistry because we dated in 2012, and it was the same guy with whom I got arrested and wasn't allowed around for a period of time. I thought he had changed and grown, but he was worse than I could have imagined. This man was emotionally and mentally abusive; he would emotionally cheat on me, then gaslight me into thinking it was nothing.

I genuinely thought I was overreacting when he'd hide messages on his phone. I loved him wholeheartedly until one night I caught him messaging other women, and he freaked out.

He was drinking while my son and niece were in bed; he even went as far as trying to get drugs delivered to my house. He took my phone so I couldn't call the cops or my dad; he made fun of my disability and was screaming heinous things about Shane to hurt me.

It was a very terrifying experience; I felt helpless, heartbroken, and disgusted in myself for ever letting this man live with me and be around my son and niece, who lived with me at the time.

I had to kick him out in the middle of the night because he wouldn't stop screaming hurtful words about Shane, but I am so thankful my son didn't hear any of it.

That whole experience traumatized me in dating. I'm always afraid to trust someone and not know their full intentions; I'm more cautious, though, which isn't necessarily a terrible thing.

Shortly after that experience, I purchased a taser, pepper spray, and a knife to protect myself. I have a knife near my bed, many areas in my home, and I never leave my place without one. He made me realize how scary people can be and how vulnerable I truly am.

I have been through a lot in my 29 years of life — things no person should ever have to endure.

I was angry for a lot of it because that was all I knew; I had to unlearn and shift my anger into compassion. I had to forgive people who couldn't, or wouldn't, say sorry, not for them but for me.

I had to forgive my mother, who didn't know how to raise me lovingly; I had to forgive my father for leaving me at a young age because he was too wrapped up in his own hurt (though he changed his life around in 2017).

I had to forgive myself for not knowing any better and letting my toxic traits seep into other people's lives. I had to forgive Shane for leaving this earth too soon and leaving Kayden without a father.

I had to forgive Meagan and the three others who paralyzed me for me to heal, and I had to find the courage within myself to accept these traumatic events and turn them into power to help someone else get through something similar, possibly.

Raising a boy without his father has been extremely hard, to say the least. After Shane died, I missed him dearly but also felt angry that he left me with a responsibility that we both agreed to: Kayden.

Once I started therapy, my therapist validated my feelings and made me feel heard, something I hadn't experienced before. Now that I'm a mom, I try to make sure my son feels heard, too. There have been times when I would yell to get my point across, but I noticed that it did more harm than good.

Instead of continuing that cycle, I looked for ways to change my approach, and I focused on the tone of my voice. I thought it was normal to get my point across by getting mad at them, and it took a long time to overcome it. It still happens sometimes, but I have gotten better at correcting myself.

I grew up around addiction; it's ruined many lives in my family, and I have seen firsthand the damage that it does.

As Kayden gets older, I will soon talk to him more in-depth about what it truly does to our people.

Addiction has run through our family for generations, and it stops with me; my son has never seen me drunk or high, and I promise that he never will. He won't feel scared in his own home because his mom is too intoxicated to look after him, he won't see the fighting and the chaos I did growing up, and I won't hit him just because I'm frustrated with him.

He is the best part of Shane and me, and I want him to grow up to become more than just a statistic. I can't change my past, but I can learn from my mistakes and my parents' mistakes so that Kayden has the best possible chance at what life has to offer.

AFTER THE IMPACT
THE DAY THAT CHANGED EVERYTHING

These photos are not easy to look at, and they were never meant to be. They capture the day my life changed forever, when a drunk driver stole my freedom and rewrote my story. I share them not for sympathy, but for truth.

I want others to see the reality behind the headlines, to understand that one careless decision can shatter lives in a heartbeat.

These images tell the part of my story that words can't fully hold — the pain, the fight, the will to live again. If sharing them saves even one life or one family from this kind of heartbreak, then every scar has served its purpose.

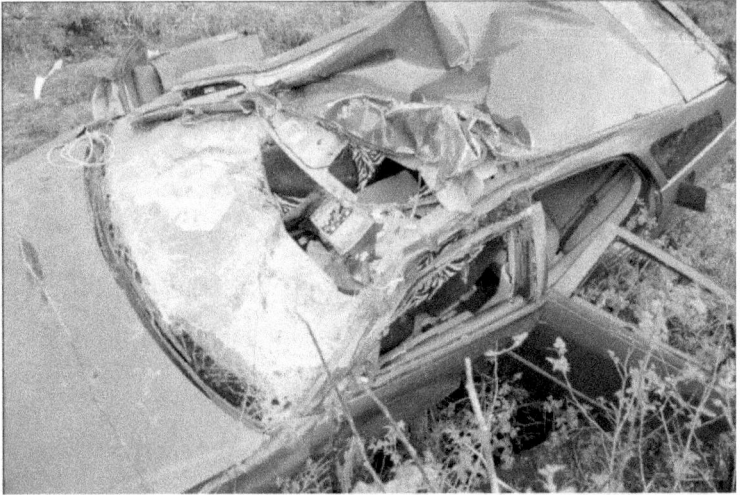

ABOUT SYDNEY MICKEY
THE STRENGTH BEHIND THE SCARS

Sydney Mickey is a proud First Nations author whose life stands as both a warning and a beacon of hope.

Raised in a small coastal town where beauty and hardship walk hand in hand, Sydney's roots run deep through generations marked by the wounds of residential schools and the strength of survival.

Her journey turned tragic when a drunk driver left her paralyzed, and her partner's suicide left her a single mother. Yet, through pain, she found her voice.

In Strength in Scars: Pain, Prison, and the Drunk Driver Who Changed Everything, Sydney writes with raw honesty about intergenerational trauma, resilience, and the power of reclaiming one's life. Her message is simple but mighty - *your scars do not define you; they refine you*.

Today, Sydney uses her words to heal, to teach, and to remind others that even in brokenness, beauty can rise again.